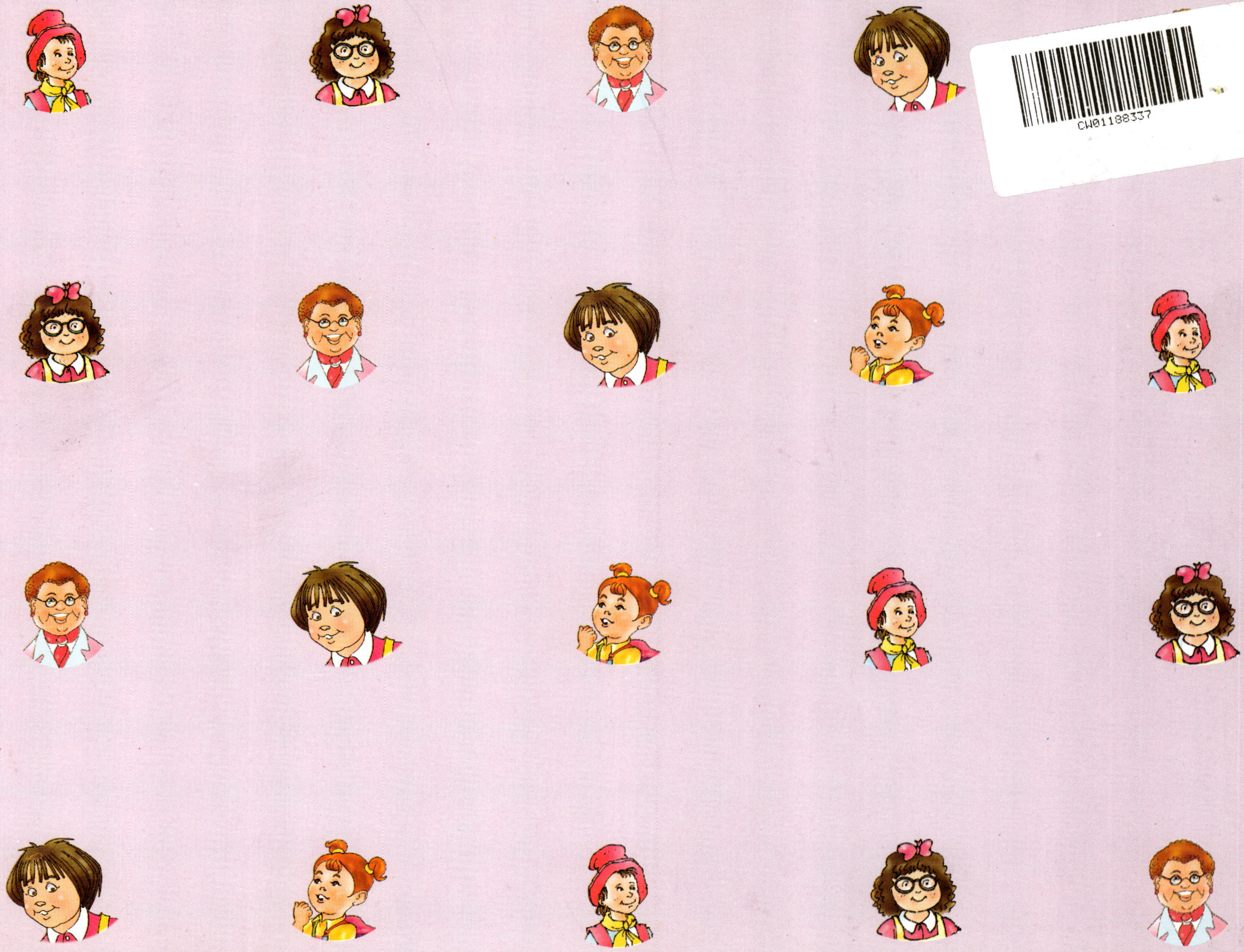

名字的含义

What's in a Name?

English – Chinese

Susan Carter

Carter, Susan
What's in a Name?
Dual language children's book

c Star Publishers Distributors
    ISBN: 81-7650-095-X

Published in India for
STAR BOOKS
55, Warren Street,
London WIT 5NW (UK)
Email: indbooks@spduk.fsnet.co.uk

by
Star Publishers Distributors
New Delhi 110002 (India)

Peacock Series
First Edition: 2004

Editor: Manju Gupta
Chinese translation by: Wan Suhai
Designing by: Dots 'N' Lines
Printed at: Public Printing (Delhi) Service

This was her first day in school. The six-year old girl stood at the door of her new class. Her face was lit up with excitement.

这是她第一天上学，这个六岁的小姑娘站在新班级门口，激动得脸上泛起了红晕。

The other children were busy playing in the room. The class-teacher looked at the little girl standing at the door. She could see that the girl was a little nervous.

别的孩子们在教室忙着玩耍，老师看了看门口站着的小姑娘。她看得出来，这个小姑娘有点紧张。

The teacher smiled at her, and said, "Welcome to the class! Come in, and please tell us your name."

老师朝她笑着说:"欢迎你来到新班级! 进来,请告诉大家你的名字。"

The little girl gave a wide smile and replied, "I have many names. I don't know which name to tell, because everyone at home calls me by a different name."

The teacher was amused. "Okay, tell us all your names," she said.

小姑娘开心地笑了，回答说："我有许多名字，不知道该说哪一个，因为家里的每个人叫我不同的名字。"

老师乐了，说："好吧，那就把你所有的名字都告诉大家吧。"

"My father calls me Bunny because he says that when I give my toothy smile, I look like a bunny rabbit," said the girl.

小姑娘说:"爸爸叫我小兔子,他说因为我笑时牙齿露出来,看上去象只兔子。"

"My mother calls me Chubby because she says she loves to pull my round cheeks."

"妈妈叫我圆圆，因为她喜欢揪我圆圆的脸蛋。"

The teacher smiled at the girl, and said, "Your mother has given you a very sweet name. I like it."

老师朝小姑娘笑了笑，说："你妈妈给你起了个很甜的名字，我喜欢这个名字。"

After a minute, the teacher asked, "Do you have grandparents?"

"Yes," the girl answered, "My grandfather lovingly calls me Peaches."

"That must be because you have a peaches and cream complexion, isn't it?" the teacher enquired.

"No," the girl explained, "it is because he loves peaches. He has even grown a peach tree in our garden."

老师停了停，问："你有爷爷奶奶吗？"

"有，"小姑娘回答说，"爷爷亲切地叫我桃子。"

老师问她："那一定是因为你的脸又细嫩又圆，象个桃子，对吧？"

"不是，"小姑娘回答道，"因为爷爷喜欢桃子，他还在园子里种了桃树呢。"

"My grandmother calls me Candy," the girl continued.
"That's an odd name!" remarked the teacher.
The girl promptly added, "Yes, but you don't know how much I love to eat peanut candy!"

小姑娘继续说道:"奶奶叫我小糖果。"

"这个名字很奇特。"老师评论说。

小姑娘突然接着说:"是很奇特,但你不知道我多么喜欢吃花生糖果。"

"What about your brother or sister?" the teacher asked.
"My brother calls me Teddy, because I cannot sleep at night without my teddy bear by my side," the girl remarked. "And my sister calls me Maddy when she gets mad at me for scribbling in her notebooks!"

老师问:"那你兄弟姐妹怎么叫你?"
"哥哥叫我熊熊,原因是,如果我的玩具熊不在身边,晚上我就闹着不睡觉,"小姑娘回答说,"姐姐叫我小胡闹,因为每当我在她的笔记本乱划时,她就气得发疯。"

"Now tell us, by what name should we call you in the class?" asked the teacher smilingly.

"You can call me Timsy. This is my real name," replied the girl.

"It is a lovely name," the teacher remarked, inviting her into the classroom.

老师笑着问她:"告诉大家,在班上我们该叫哪个名字?"

小姑娘回答说:"大家就叫我蒂姆西吧,这是我的正式名字。"

老师说:"好可爱的名字。"便请她进教室。

Timsy stood in the doorway and did not move. "What is it Timsy? Why don't you come in?" the teacher asked.

"I want to know your name first," Timsy responded.

蒂姆西站在门口不动。老师便问:"蒂姆西,怎么啦?为什么不进来?"

蒂姆西回答说:"我想先知道您的名字。"

The teacher smiled at the curious little girl, and replied, "Like you, I too have many names."

All the children turned to look at their teacher in surprise.

老师对这个好奇的姑娘笑了，回答道："我和你一样，也有很多名字。"

所有的孩子都吃惊地看着老师。

The teacher broke into a loud laughter. "I will tell you all the names I have. I am sure you will find them as interesting as yours," she said.

老师突然大声笑了。"我会告诉你我的所有名字，我相信你会觉得它们和你的名字一样有趣。"

The teacher continued, "My niece and nephew call me Auntie, because I am their father's sister. They are very naughty, and want me to play games with them all the time."

老师接着说:"我的侄子们叫我姑姑,因为我是他们父亲的妹妹。他们很调皮,老要我陪他们玩。"

"Do you know what my children call me at home? My son calls me Mum. I feel he thinks that I talk too much, and wants me to keep quiet!" she remarked amusingly.

"你知道在家里我的孩子们叫我什么吗？我儿子叫我妈姆。他觉得我说话太多，要我保持沉默。"老师逗乐地说。

"I have two grandchildren, who always want me to take them to the market to buy toys. They call me Grandma," she said.

老师说："我有两个孙子，他们总缠着我，要我到市场上给他们买玩具。 他们叫我奶奶。"

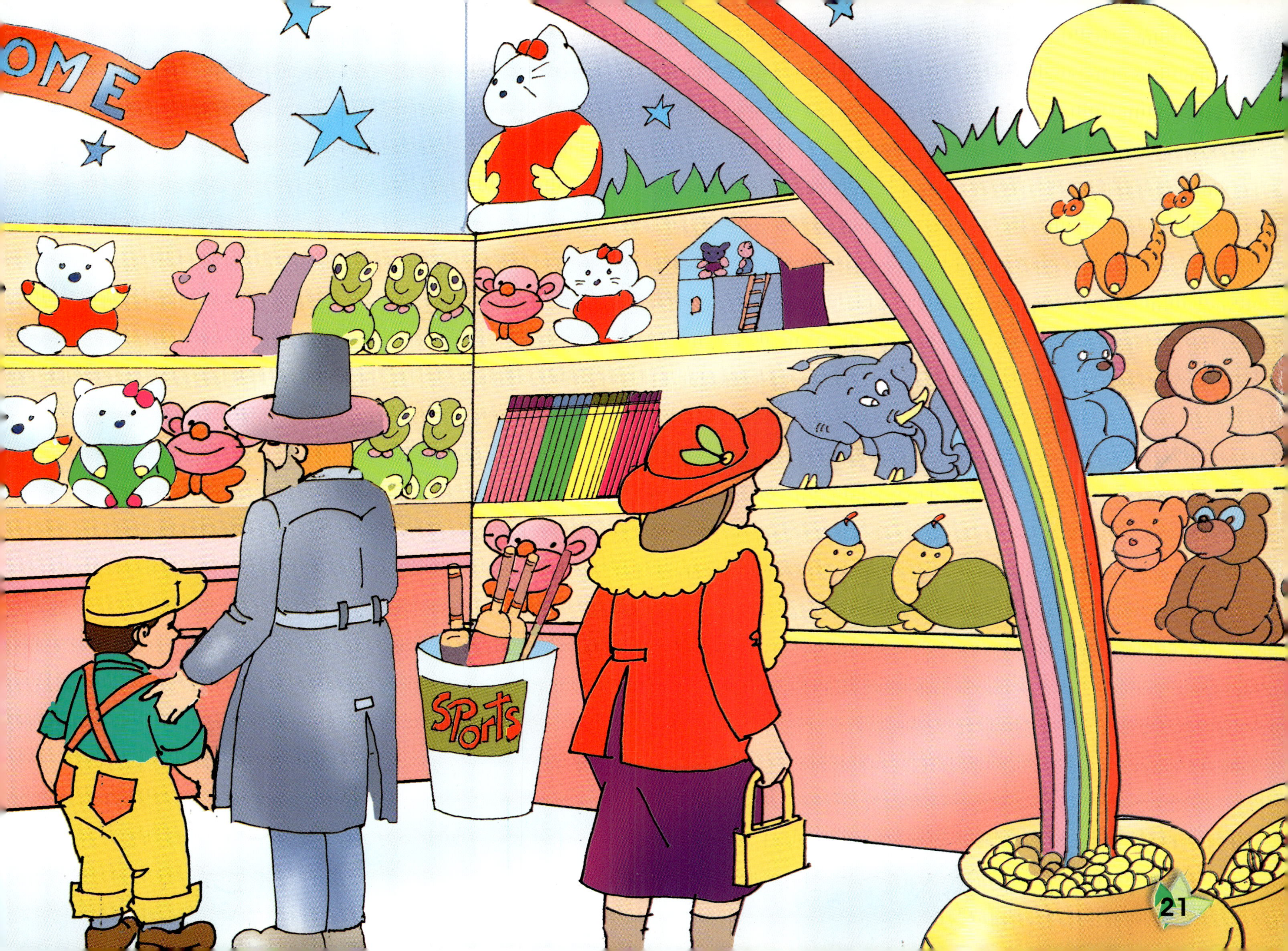
OME
Sports

"My neighbours call me Mrs. Robinson. You know why? That's because this is my surname," she explained.

"邻居们叫我罗伯逊夫人。你知道为什么吗？因为这是我的姓。"老师解释说。

"But what is your real name?" Timsy asked.
The teacher answered, "My real name is Kelly. Do you like it?"
"Yes, I like it very much," Timsy replied promptly.

蒂姆西问:"那你的正式名字叫什么?"

老师回答说:"我的正式名字叫凯丽,你喜欢这个名字吗?"

蒂姆西很干脆地回答说:"喜欢,我很喜欢这个名字。"

Do you know why Timsy likes her teacher's name? That's because Timsy calls her favourite teddy bear by the name of Kelly!

你知道为什么蒂姆西喜欢老师的名字吗？原来她把最喜爱的熊玩具也叫凯丽。

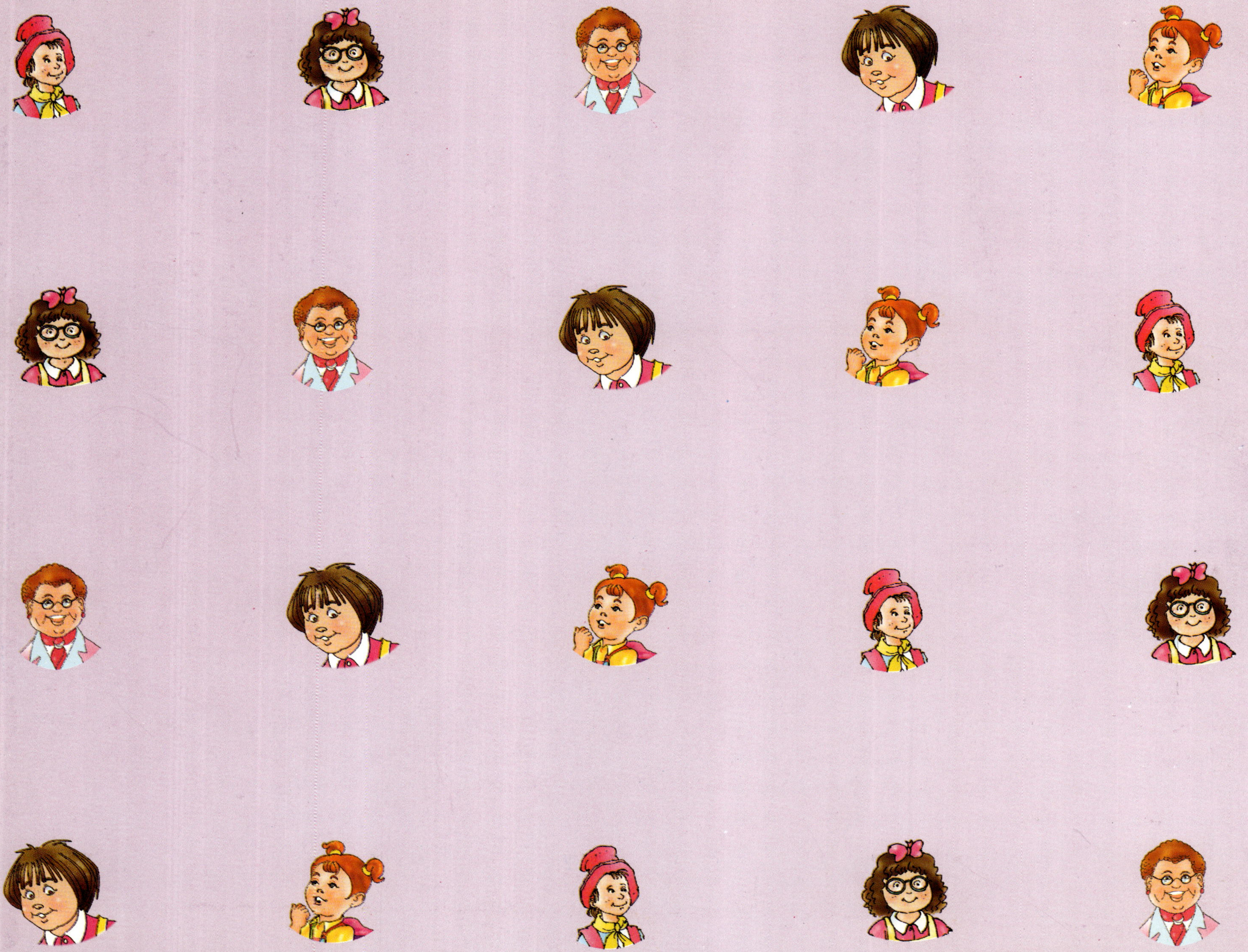